The Gypsy and the Candy Floss Queen

The Gypsy and the Candy Floss Queen

George Jowett

Smokestack Books
1 Lake Terrace, Grewelthorpe, Ripon HG4 3BU
e-mail: info@smokestack-books.co.uk
www.smokestack-books.co.uk

ISBN 978-1-9161392-0-6

Smokestack Books
is represented
by Inpress Ltd

For my brave, brilliant
and beautiful daughters,
Laura, Amy, Lucy,
Rosie and Georgie.

'Bein' a dad, isn't so bad...'
Loudon Wainwright III

Contents

Preface

I suspect that two obvious questions will suggest themselves to readers of *The Gypsy and the Candy Floss Queen*. Firstly, why would anyone choose to write a murder mystery in verse? And secondly why, if they had to attempt such a thing, would they take as their subject an unsolved murder from nearly forty years ago, and one in which not only the victim, but the chief suspect and nearly all the major players in the case are long dead?

I've always wanted to try my hand at a whodunnit. I've been a fan of crime fiction since childhood when I read my first Sherlock Holmes and Father Brown stories, and my admiration and respect for modern crime writers like Val McDermid, Ian Rankin, Peter Robinson and Ann Cleeves, knows no bounds.

I know I couldn't do what these stars of the genre do. I don't possess a novelist's gifts. I'm not a 'proper writer' and would struggle with plot, character and dialogue. What I am is a competent versifier, so if I write a whodunnit, I'm afraid it'll have to be in verse. I'm not the first to attempt the feat. The late HRF Keating tried to do it with *Jack, the Lady Killer*. Keating was a good writer and a fine novelist. He won the CWA's Diamond Dagger in 1996, but sadly what he wasn't was a skilled poet. His attempt to write his fictional crime story in Pushkin sonnets is, for me, a failure and before I'd finished reading the first part of his story it was perfectly obvious who'd done it; indeed within the first few stanzas it was clear the author, on his own admission, had failed to master the verse form and would go on to murder it completely.

I first read about the case of the Gypsy and the Candy Floss Queen during Lawrence Wood's trial at Teesside Crown court in the summer of 1979, in the *Northern Echo.* I remember being intrigued by the titillating, salacious details, and later, by the astounding outcome when, after a two week long trial, the defendant was finally acquitted.

Unsurprisingly, my memory of the case quickly faded, and I doubt whether I would have recollected it at all, had I not happened to notice a report, in the same daily paper, nearly thirty years later, of Lawrence Wood's suicide. It seemed strange and incongruous that the handsome, carefree, young gypsy of the earlier case had chosen to end his days, by his own hand, in the back of his battered, old Ford transit van, and immediately my interest and suspicions were aroused.

Eventually, five years later, someone succeed in re-booting my poetic hard-drive and once I'd begun processing words again, my thoughts soon returned to the case. Indeed, events in the summer of 2013 conspired to draw me powerfully back to it.

I remember in particular one Saturday evening in June. I was sitting in my car outside the pizza shop where I worked as a delivery driver, when my mobile rang. It was my eldest daughter, ringing to tell me that, earlier in the day, her sister Amy had been injured and taken to hospital during an anti-fascist demonstration in Westminster. The protest, Unite Against Fascism, had been called to frustrate attempts by right-wing groups, including the BNP and EDL, to make political capital in the aftermath of the murder of Trooper Lee Rigby. My daughter had been in the vanguard of the anti-fascist protestors when one of the officers policing the rally had singled her out for no real reason, other than that she, as a defenceless woman exercising her democratic rights, rather than a tattooed, shaven-headed, foul-mouthed, belligerent extremist looking for trouble, represented the easy option. The officer concerned suddenly began kicking her repeatedly and with excessive force on her knee joint, causing what the doctors call a 'bumper fracture' and inflicting life-changing injuries. As a result, she was hospitalized for weeks, and over the next eighteen months underwent repeated bouts of reconstructive surgery.

I remembered my own experience of violence, though of a less severe nature, at the hands of the police when, as a fifteen year old, I'd been beaten up by officers as they'd broken up our peaceful, unofficial 'legalize pot' rally on Primrose Hill in the mid 1960s. I remembered too the shocking, scandalous 'unexplained' death of David Oluwale in 1969 when I was a student at Leeds Polytechnic. A few years later, when I was studying in Newcastle to become a social worker, the late Ralph Bell, then vicar of Otterburn and the father of Tim, one of my best friends on the course, led the campaign for an independent inquiry in to the death in custody of Liddle Towers in Gateshead.

It suddenly occurred to me then that the story of the Gypsy and the Candy Floss Queen would be the perfect vehicle through which to articulate and explore my own sense of anger, outrage and injustice at the apparent fact that the police have been getting away with murder, both metaphorically and sometimes, shockingly, even literally, for most of my lifetime.

The Gypsy and the Candy Floss Queen

'*It was only a gypsy*
A ragged, shaggy blackguard of a didecoy
Up to no good I did what I should
A little physical persuasion and he passed on by...'
Jake Thackray

Part One

1

It's six a.m. The day's beginning.
A man is walking up the lane.
Inside the hedge songbirds are singing.
He sniffs, he stops, then sniffs again.
Can he smell smoke? To be explicit
A bonfire? The allotments, is it?
Well something's burning, and he'd say
It isn't all that far away.
His pace along the lane now quickens,
He turns the corner, sees the blaze,
The pall of smoke, the shimmering haze.
The sight before him shocks and sickens
-A burning Morris motor car.
Its blistered paint begins to char.

2

The heat's intense. He can't get nearer
To see if anyone's inside.
He squints, he peers, but gets no clearer
Impression so he then decides
He'd better summon some assistance.
Recalling passing in the distance
A phone box in the empty street
He turns, and now on hurrying feet,
Heads back towards the village running.
Just minutes later, panting, hot,
He stands inside that very spot,
He gasps for breath, he's all but done in,
Dials 999. 'Which Service, please?'
'The Fire Brigade and the Police…'

3

The fire at last has been extinguished
And a discovery's soon made.
A smell like roast pork was distinguished
As the fire crew worked. Some, dismayed,
Said, 'I swear that's a body burning!'
Grim-faced and with their stomachs churning
They peer into the smouldering car.
'Aye, look, I told you. There you are!'
All black and burned. Could it be human,
A body as it is alleged,
Between the back and front seats wedged?
The youngest takes a look. 'It's true, man.'
He pales then retches. 'Oh my God,
What should we do?' 'Wait for the Plod.'

4

Now at the lane end, like a sentry,
A constable stands at his post.
The lane's been closed off. There's no entry.
It's now a crime scene it's supposed.
The firemen stand on one side waiting
While officers investigating
The facts try to establish who
The victim is. They have one clue.
Still legible, the registration
Of the car is radioed in.
Police enquiries begin.
The search for any information
Is underway. Soon, slow but sure,
A team will go from door to door.

5

The Murder Squad has taken over.
The victim's been identified.
It didn't take long to discover
Who she was, but why she died
(For that's in fact their stated mission)
Could be a different proposition.
One thing is crystal clear at least,
Miriam Culine, the deceased,
Had led a colourful existence,
Or so the rumours would suggest.
With Youth and Beauty amply blessed
She'd got herself, with their assistance,
A husband older than herself,
One quite well off, but in poor health.

6

At seventeen, a pastor's daughter,
She'd run away and joined a fair,
Worked on the show grounds. There they'd taught her
To run a stall. She'd learned to share
The lifestyle of the travelling showmen,
And like lots of attractive women
She hadn't even had to try
To catch the fairground boss's eye.
With her he'd soon become enamoured,
He was besotted, taken in,
Her beauty had him in a spin.
His old heart in his chest had hammered
As, helplessly, beneath her spell,
The fairground king, Fred Culine, fell.

7

His Queen of Candy Floss he'd call her.
She laughed at that, so Fred began
To woo her, hoping to install her
As queen too in his caravan.
At first, resisting him demurely,
She shook her head, but slowly, surely,
As Fred continued his campaign
With flowers, chocolates and champagne,
He overcame all her objections,
Convinced her it would be alright,
And finally, to his delight,
He'd won a place in her affections.
Yes, she'd agreed she would move in,
Their life together could begin.

8

'The old fool!' as response was standard.
'Never? He didn't? What, they'll wed?'
'He's old enough to be her grandad!'
That's what a lot of people said.
But others laughed and thought it fair dos
That young brunettes with bouffant hair-dos
Should use their charms and all their art
To do well in the marriage mart.
Fred's family weren't pleased or cheerful.
His grown-up nephews, fearful lest
By his wife they'd be dispossessed,
Behind his back, gave her an earful.
'Gold-digger! Mercenary cow!'
They'd never get Fred's money now.

9

And if they could they would have stopped her.
They couldn't, and the couple wed
A while ago. Now someone's topped her
Those nephews who all wished her dead?
They're in the frame there's no denying,
But so's the man they're notifying
As next of kin of his wife's death.
Poor Fred, who's old and short of breath,
Insists, although they're separated
And she has her own caravan,
She's still his wife, he's still her man.
Whatever's been insinuated
He loves her and they get on well.
But is it true? It's hard to tell

10

Fred Culine could have killed his missus.
Why would he tell the cops the truth?
The Chief Super remains suspicious,
But knows he hasn't any proof.
The argument keeps on revolving.
The Chief's no closer yet to solving
The mystery of why she died.
Forensic science has supplied
The hard facts. She'd been knocked out, senseless,
Then stripped, not bare, but to her bra,
Shoved in the back seat of her car
And left, unconscious and defenceless.
The killer then set it alight
And disappeared into the night.

11

Not Fred perhaps. He's old and ailing,
Incapable of such an act;
He's doddery; his health is failing
Too frail to hurt a fly in fact.
But if he didn't kill her, who did?
The suspects on the list included
The show folk, all who'd worked for Fred,
For knowing he would wish her dead
One of them might, to curry favour
Or do himself a bit of good
And guarantee his livelihood,
Have done her in. A thought to savour
For the Chief. Possible? Well yes,
But likely? He can only guess.

12

There's lots to look at; facts to order;
New angles to find out about.
His focus keeps on getting broader
And each new lead needs teasing out.
And so enquiries continue.
The Murder Squad strain nerve and sinew
Re-covering the same old ground,
Collating everything they've found;
Re-interviewing friends, relations
In search of the one break they need,
The crucial clue they hope will lead
Them to the final revelation
And in the end provide the key
To the killer's identity.

Part Two

13

A new name comes to the attention
Of the police, one Lawrence Wood.
(A man of whom there's been no mention
Till now, although perhaps there should.)
Miriam's 'friend'. Some are suggesting
Her close friend. Will the cops be testing
How close precisely? Oh, you bet,
More details they'll be keen to get!
They'll grill poor Lawrence Wood severely.
'Now what's your part in this young man?
Tell us how this affair began?
Come on now.' They'll stare at him queerly.
'Answer our questions, Mr Wood.
Let's have the truth for your own good.'

14

For him they'll have questions aplenty.
They'll try the good cop/bad cop ploy
On Lawrence, who is just turned twenty,
A handsome, dark-eyed Gypsy boy.
Suspicious of police, distrusting
(The cops think didicois disgusting
As Lawrence knows only too well)
Why can't they all just go to hell?
The interview for him's a trial.
It takes place in his caravan
In Wingate. He does what he can
To stall them with a flat denial.
'I haven't seen her for eight weeks.'
They write his words down as he speaks.

15

But Lawrence, frightened, naïve, youthful,
Is sadly just about to make,
By being rather less than truthful,
A grave and serious mistake.
He'd actually seem Mrs Culine
The night she'd died. His hopes of fooling
The coppers aren't exactly high
But he sees no choice but to try.
So Lawrence makes the wrong decision,
Gives answers that are far from straight,
Designed simply to obfuscate,
For if he made a frank admission
Of where he'd been and at what time
He fears they'd charge him with the crime.

16

'Alright I can't deny I knew her,
Nor that we had a brief affair.
And yes, it's true, I used to screw her
But not for eight months now, I swear.
I've got a new love, Edith Flowers,
A pub landlady. I spend hours
With her these days. Am I a what?
A womaniser? No, I'm not.
A ladies' man? Well, not that I know.
It wouldn't mean 'owt if I was.
How's that? I'll tell you how, because
I'd never do that to her. Why no,
I'd loved her. She was kind and sweet.
A nicer girl you couldn't meet.'

17

The cops seem happy with his story.
They must believe it to be true,
And as they leave, he's pretty sure he
Has done the best that he can do.
He couldn't tell the truth now, could he?
'Your trousers are a little muddy,'
Observes one DC at the door.
Lawrence looks down. 'They are, for sure.'
'Been out?' suggests the surlier one.
Young Lawrence nods as he replies
'Took dogs out for some exercise.'
'And when was this?' 'Oh, earlier on.'
'And where exactly did you go?'
'Oh, round the fields and woods, you know.'

18

'And who's the girlfriend now, remind me?'
'It's Edith.' 'At the Queen's Head?' 'Aye,
That's right. Most days that's where you'll find me.'
'We'll leave it there for now. Goodbye.'
Poor Lawrence can't believe they're going,
And though he has no way of knowing
Their thoughts, he hopes they've bought his tale.
But soon his nerve begins to fail.
Uncertainty and doubt affect him.
They climb into their car while he
Stares at them rather anxiously.
He's positive that they suspect him.
No doubt they'll put him in the frame.
He wonders who gave them his name?

19

Next night, they're back. Another visit.
They hammer on his van's front door.
'Not you again? And now what is it?
This time what do you want me for?'
'We've come to take you to the station.'
'More questions and interrogation?'
'The Super wants to have a chat.'
'But what about?' 'Oh, this and that.'
'I've told you all I know already.'
(He knows he's told a pack of lies.)
'We've found a few discrepancies.'
His legs seem suddenly unsteady.
They're on to him! He fears that's it.
He knows now he's deep in the shit.

20

'If you won't come voluntarily
We'll just arrest you.' Shell-shocked, numb,
Lawrence pauses momentarily,
Then answers 'No, of course I'll come.
I'll get me jacket.' 'We'll come with you.'
They follow him inside. 'And if you
Can find them trousers that you wore
With mud on...' 'That's them, on the floor.'
He holds them up for their inspection.
'Yes, they're the ones. Put them in this.
They'll be sent for analysis.
I take it you've got no objections?'
Lawrence shrugs, then shakes his head.
He's hardly heard a word they've said.

21

They take him to the waiting panda.
One sits beside him in the back
And whispers with surprising candour
'It's time, my lad, to face the flack.'
Poor Lawrence, anxious and befuddled,
His thoughts disjointed and all muddled,
Stays silent as the road unwinds,
Till finally at last he finds
They've stopped outside Police Headquarters.
His escort quickly takes him in,
A new nightmare will now begin.
They lead him like a lamb to slaughter.
'Oh, Mr Wood? For interview?
I'll tell the Super. Take him through.'

22

The cops don't seem in any hurry.
Young Lawrence, twiddling his thumbs
Is left to sit and wait and worry
Till the Superintendent comes.
Like Odysseus on Ithaca,
Chief Superintendent Whittaker
Has not even been sighted yet.
He's happy to let Lawrence sweat
Until the little room is humming.
Yes, let the suspect sit and stew
In his own juice an hour or two.
He thinks it makes them more forthcoming.
The longer that they sit and wait
The better they'll co-operate.

23

Well that's what Clayton's always reckoned,
And though it seems a strange idea
It's served him when promotion's beckoned,
And served him well. It's pretty clear
As a detective he's successful.
He never finds it hard or stressful
And nearly always gets his man.
(He has since his career began).
In short, he is the perfect copper.
The proof of his ability?
He's now the head of CID.
He couldn't, could he, come a cropper?
His self-belief and pride's immense.
His weakness? Overconfidence.

24

'You'll need a solicitor, Lawry,
A legal representative.
You'll have the name of yours? No? Sorry?
You haven't got one. Oh well, if
You'd like to pick one from the roster,
Today there's Messrs Gray or Foster.
We'll give the one you choose a call.
Pick either. Each will do their all.
No, I can't help to do the choosing.
You think you'll go for Mr Gray?
That's fine. We'll call him right away.
You're sure now he's the one you're using?
We can't begin until he's here.
How long exactly? No idea.'

25

A hurried confab with his client
When Mr Gray arrives takes place
From which it's clear just how reliant
On lies is his young client's case.
'But did you do it?' 'No, sir, truly
I didn't.' Mr Gray now coolly
Explains their bold new strategy.
'Just tell the truth. Believe you me,
You've been busily excavating
Your own grave, and though perhaps I
Can understand the reason why,
Yet our best chance of extricating
You from this mess, as we've discussed
Is through the truth. The truth's a must.'

26

Poor Lawrence visibly is wincing.
He's struggling with Gray's advice.
'I see you need some more convincing
But lying isn't ever wise
In answer to a copper's questions.
I think you'll find that my suggestion
Will serve you better in the end.
It may be hard to comprehend,
But otherwise they'll think you're lying
Because you're guilty or involved.
For them the case is half-way solved.
I'm sorry, Lawrence, but I'm trying
To make it really plain to you
The damage all these lies can do.'

27

He's right about the consequences.
They are just as he has outlined,
For as the interview commences
Lawrence is quite surprised to find
His words of yesterday are quoted,
The words the officer had noted.
' ' I haven't seen her for eight weeks'
-That's what you said.' The Super speaks,
'It's not the truth, though, Lawrence, is it?'
'No, sir.' 'So you admit you lied?'
'I do.' 'In fact the night she died
You'd paid Mrs Culine a visit,
Hadn't you?' Lawrence looks glum, 'I had.'
'That's better,' the Chief smiles. 'Now lad

28

Tell us what happened when you saw her.'
'I went round 'cos she asked me to.'
'You found you'd still got feelings for her?'
'Well, no, that really isn't true.
No, I've moved on. I love another.
Edith Flowers is my new lover.'
'Jealous, was she? Get out of hand?'
'It didn't. You don't understand.
You make it sound furtive and grubby.'
'Well tell us how it really was.'
'Miriam asked me round because
She wanted to escape her hubby.
She'd money, but not quite enough.
She wanted me to sell some stuff,

29

Jewellery and that.' 'Oh, give us credit!'
The Super snorts in disbelief.
'That's just baloney. I'd have said it
Is far more likely you're a thief,
And that you killed her for her jewellery.
So, Lawrence, stop all this tomfoolery,
I simply haven't got the time.
For fantasies. This brutal crime,
It isn't some detective thriller,
No, this is real life, this is fact.
I think you did this dreadful act.
Is that what happened? Did you kill her,
Then steal her bracelets, rings, her gold?
Come on. It's time the truth was told.'

30

'I've told the truth. She asked to see me.
She'd had enough of threats from Fred.
'Oh Lawrence, will you help to free me,
Help me escape?' That's what she said.
She'd been my lover you must remember.
It only finished last November
When Fred found out. It had to end.
But Miriam was still my friend,
So, when she asked me to assist her
Escaping from that man's abuse
There was no way I could refuse.
We were like brother and like sister.
That's what most people thought we were
Last week in Jedburgh, me and her.'

31

'I'm sorry? Jedburgh? When, exactly
Were you in Jedburgh?' 'Just last week,
Thursday, was it?' Matter of factly
Lawrence ponders. A strangled shriek
Of anger and of irritation
From Clayton greets this information.
'So you and she had a day out
In Jedburgh? What was that about
And what precisely were you doing?'
'A new site for her caravan
Was what she sought. She had a plan,
One she was actively pursuing
-It was to get away from Fred
And make a fresh start, as I've said.'

32

'Twice in a week you met the victim?'
'Well yes, sir, I suppose I did.'
The Super has a simple dictum:
The truth is like a dustbin lid.
It's there, in your face. It's obvious
The suspect's lying; he's devious.
To Clayton what these 'facts' suggest
Is what he has already guessed,
That Lawrence is the perpetrator.
He must be. Why else would he lie?
Well, gypsies do. Though he'll deny.
He did it, Clayton's sure that later
They'll charge young Lawrence with the crime.
Case solved and closed in record time.

33

And just as well, the Super muses
For he's two killers now to catch.
From Darlington today the news is
Another murder on his patch.
For that reason he particularly
Needs to get this one sown up quickly.
But Clayton's certain now he will.
He's getting closer to the kill.
The gypsy boy's a poor opponent.
He hasn't the intelligence,
The cunning or the common sense,
While Clayton is a skilled proponent
Of the interrogative art.
He'll pick the gypsy's tale apart.

34

On that he must now focus solely.
He knows there is no other way
As, like a lion, stalking slowly
He creeps up on his frightened prey.
'So take me back to Monday, would you?
Now, Lawrence, if I've understood you
What you were saying was that she
Asked you to sell some jewellery?'
'That's right. And some Crown Derby china.'
'Some china too? And all good stuff?'
'She needed funds.' 'That's fair enough.'
Clayton's smile couldn't be benigner.
'But why on earth would she ask you
To do a job that she could do?'

35

'Some of the stuff her Fred had bought her.
She couldn't sell it locally.
If Fred had seen it or had caught her,
Her plans were scuppered totally.
If he got wind there would be ructions,
So Miriam gave me instructions
To sell it somewhere far away.
And that is what I did next day
In Lingdale. There, a garage owner
(Aye, Lingdale, near to Saltburn sands)
Took all the jewellery off my hands.
And that's the truth upon my honour.'
'In Lingdale then, this deal was done?
On Tuesday afternoon just gone?

36

The day the murder was committed?
The same day that you told my men
You hadn't seen her?' 'I've admitted
I lied....' 'You've lied, then lied again!'
Now Clayton seems exasperated.
'Your story is invalidated
By all your falsehoods and deceit.
In fact, I'd say it's all complete
Bollocks. Yes, it's disingenuous,
Designed to baffle and confuse.
But Lawrence, sadly it's no use.
Your grasp on truth may be tenuous,
But some of us see through the murk
Created round your dirty work'

37

Now Mr Gray tries interceding.
'My client is prepared to make
A statement.' 'That should make good reading.
I tell you what, let's have a break
And then we'll take down his dictation.
I have to say my expectation
Is that there's every likelihood
We'll soon be charging Mr Wood.
With what? With murdering Miriam.
There is no evidence to link
Him with the crime? That's what you think.
Am I serious? You bet I am!
It's circumstantial? Maybe, but
I've got this feeling in my gut.'

38

Impossible he is mistaken.
That iron certainty's not feigned.
So once his statement has been taken
Young Lawrence Wood will be arraigned,
(As Clayton has already hinted)
Charged with her murder, finger-printed,
Then read his rights (you know the script),
And of all his possessions stripped,
(Belt and shoe-laces confiscated,)
Be locked up till he can be brought
Before the Magistrates in Court
Next day, when it's anticipated
The prisoner will quickly be
Remanded into custody.

Part Three

39

A year on, Lawrence, the defendant,
In pinstripe suit, sits in the dock,
Flanked by two warders, his attendants.
They listen as the judge takes stock,
Reiterating for the jury
The details of the tangled story
They've heard. Yes, Mr Justice Jupp
Is busy with his summing up.
But oh how slowly it progresses.
'You've heard the prosecution make....'
It's hard sometimes to stay awake
As, in great detail, he addresses
The issues to be clarified,
The things the jury must decide.

40

'Your role is not investigation.
Your task is simply to decide
If, after due consideration
And on the evidence supplied...'
(His syntax *is* circumlocution)
'...The case put by the prosecution
Is proven. You must think about
Beyond all reasonable doubt
And what that means. Are you persuaded
The case the prosecution made
The simple facts clearly displayed?
And is what happened what they say did?
Is Lawrence Wood a murderer?
On that the jury must confer.

41

No other question should detain you.
Who did it if not Mr Wood
Need not concern or entertain you.
I hope that's clearly understood?
That's not for you. In fact I'd deem it
Goes well beyond your proper remit.
No, that's one for the CID,
For plainly it's their territory
On which you mustn't go trespassing.
Stick to the evidence reviewed.
Has it correctly been construed?
Your proper role is in assessing
The case that has been put to you.
Do you believe it to be true?'

42

His summing up at last completed
Judge Jupp invites them to retire,
An invitation which is greeted
(Although it's been their heart's desire
For the last few hours) with disbelief
At first, then with symptoms of relief.
'The Court will now adjourn. All rise.'
To hide his smile the foreman tries.
For them this moment's liberating,
But not for Lawrence Wood, alas.
As one by one the jurors pass
En route to their deliberating,
The poor defendant turns to go
Back to the cells to wait below.

43

'Bah, juries!' he thinks with derision.
It's been four hours. How can they take
This long in reaching a decision?
'Come on, come on for pity's sake.
This waiting could be instrumental
In driving me completely mental!'
Small wonder he feels ill at ease.
'Oh, hurry up you bastards, please.'
But straightaway Lawrence, repenting
His outburst, pleads, 'Forgive me, I'm
Just overwrought. You take your time.'
On his demand for haste relenting,
He implies they can take all night
If in the end they get it right.

44

But will they? That's the question really.
What will the jurors make of it?
They'd take his side, of course, ideally.
But might they do the opposite?
Supposing their view is distorted,
And that to them the facts are sorted
– The case the prosecution put
Seeming to them open and shut?
It couldn't, could it? Well, his sense is
It's quite impossible to say.
It might in fact go either way,
But musing on the consequences
For him, it's no surprise to find,
Does nothing for his state of mind.

45

'They're back!' at last the cry advising
The jury has returned rings out.
It doesn't end his agonizing
Or his uncertainty or doubt.
But as he climbs that spiral staircase
Up to the dock, there seems a fair case
For arguing that the ascent
Helps lessen to a small extent
His dread and his preoccupation.
He's strangely calm now as he stands
To listen as the Clerk demands
If, after due deliberation,
The jury's verdict is agreed?
Will Lawrence be sent down or freed?

46

'Do you find the defendant guilty
Or not guilty?' A moment's pause.
'Not guilty.' Justice's scales tilt. He
Is exonerated. His cause
Has triumphed. Lawrence didn't do it!
Plainly the prosecution blew it.
They had the wrong man you may think.
Forensically there was no link
Between the crime scene and defendant.
No fibre from his clothes, no mud,
No hairs and not one drop of blood.
In fact, their whole case seemed dependent
On nods and winks and facts massaged.
'Let the defendant be discharged.'

47

Now as the trial finally closes
With Lawrence freed (to his delight),
Chief Whittaker, when asked, supposes
Unless new facts should come to light,
The police will not be pursuing
The matter further, or reviewing
It. He can't see that all along
His view of things was simply wrong.
Or else he can, but daren't admit it.
How could he? He would look a clown.
There's no way Clayton can back down.
Not now. His pride will not permit it.
It means the killer won't be caught,
But somehow he'll live with that thought.

48

So to his error Clayton's blinded.
The top brass though at first demur,
But pretty soon they too are minded
To drop the case. They all concur.
Their objections proved temporary
When, weeks later, a coronary
Had felled Fred Culine, Fairground King.
He would not add a single thing
To what he had already stated.
The circumstances won't allow
Fred's cross examination now,
For his remains have been cremated.
And so as Clayton had supposed
The Culine case will remain closed.

49

The only reason I've now raised it
Is something brought it back to mind.
You would have thought time had erased it
And I was quite surprised to find
How much of it remained embedded
Inside my head, and still unshredded.
The memory of what occurred,
Of what I'd read about and heard
Was vivid still. I recollected
How I'd been thrilled by it, appalled,
Amused, astounded and enthralled
-God, what a tale, now resurrected
By news that Lawrence Wood had died,
Apparently a suicide.

50

Our local paper ran the story:
MAN'S BODY FOUND IN FUME-FILLED VAN
And then a brief, potted history
Beneath the stark headline began,
Recalling, rather mischievously,
How twenty six years previously
Lawrence's lover had been slain.
That brought it all to life again
– The crime, the trial, his acquittal,
But could it really be that he
To mark that anniversary
Had killed himself? A non-committal
Je ne sais pas is my response,
For after all he'd loved her once.

51

But there are other explanations
Which you may find have more appeal,
Fit better with your inclinations
And seem more likely and more real.
For instance, for a different ending
Try rumoured further charges pending,
Involving sex and under age
Girls, in so far as I can gauge.
Does that provoke your indignation?
Disgusting? Awful? 'Oh that's vile.
The gypsy was a paedophile!'
How's that for a humiliation?
Enough to drive a desperate man
To make the only choice he can?

52

Yes? Your answer's categorical?
I thought it was, but wait a bit.
The offences are historical,
Alleged and all unproven. It
Is far too soon to be assuming
The man was guilty. You're presuming
His death was an acknowledgment
Of guilt? But might it not have meant
Instead that Lawrence had concluded
Already that his goose was cooked,
And he, to put it bluntly, fucked?
That option cannot be excluded
For Lawrence knew a thing or two
Of how they work, the Boys in Blue.

53

He knew that they were out to get him,
And that no matter what the 'crime',
There would be no way they would let him
Just wriggle off the hook this time.
No Lawrence feared that his comeuppance
Was overdue. He'd not give tuppence
For his chances. His fate approached.
The witnesses were primed and coached.
The plot towards its resolution
Was moving swiftly. Could he slow
Or halt its progress, stop the show?
He could. But what a grim solution
– For him there'd be no curtain call.
His final act? To end it all.

54

He felt he had no other option,
No alternative, no Plan B
He could put forward for adoption.
No other course that he could see
Would save him from what now awaited,
Too awful to be contemplated
– Banged up again, as he's been once,
But branded this time as a nonce.
Too cynical my view perhaps is?
You can't accept those are the facts?
That's not how the police force acts?
There may be isolated lapses
But generally they're fair and try
To do their best. That's your reply?

55

How hopelessly idealistic!
You surely can't mean all that stuff?
It's naïve and unrealistic.
(By now that should be clear enough.)
Of course poor Lawrence was their victim.
It's pretty plain too, why they picked him.
It settled an outstanding score.
Revenge it was, of that I'm sure.
The police are quite notorious
(And no pretence, please, at surprise)
For stitch-ups, cover-ups and lies.
Their conduct's often inglorious,
Corrupt and brutal, to their shame,
And always keen to dodge the blame.

56

Just think of Hillsborough and the mothers
Who lost sons in that tragedy;
Of Azelle Rodney and the others
Who've died in police custody.
Think Tomlinson and Steven Lawrence.
No wonder we look with abhorrence
On coppers, call them 'Filth' and 'Pig.'
Towers, DeMenezes, Peach, Rigg,
Duggan, Orchard and Oluwale
Will all attest that fascist swine
And racists man that thin blue line.
The facts will out eventually,
But till they do perhaps we should
Add to that roll call Lawrence Wood?

Paradise Lost

'Right,' he said, slowly looking round the class,
'Who'd like to read?' A good joke that,
No need to ask. No-one made a sound.
All gone to ground, we kept our heads well down
And prayed he wouldn't pick on us.
'I don't know, all this fuss...'
He shook his head and chose a name at random,
'Williams, perhaps you'd like to begin?'
Poor Williams couldn't win.
He knew that question couched a clear command.
And, after a moment's pause,
Made the customary hesitant start.
'Of man's first disobedience and the fruit
Of that forbidden tree whose mortal taste....'
The lines ran on or rather crawled
As Williams dragged them after him,
'Sing Heavenly Muse, that on the secret top of... of –'
Oreb brought him to a stop.
'Of Oreb, lad' the master said.
'Of Oreb,' said young Williams, hurrying on.
'That on the secret top of Oreb....'
He somehow made it through another seven lines.
'Thank you. That's fine.' Williams smiled gratefully,
Safe in the knowledge his days suffering was done
And someone else's turn had come.
We knew it too and held our breath
Until the teacher's choice was made.
'Johnson, would you take over?'
And so in slow instalments the reading
Faltered round the class.

We never reached Book Three
Nor glimpsed that rumoured Paradise for which
The Arch Fiend's flight was bound. Instead,
Bogged down in Chaos for a term or two we stuck,
Perplexed and baffled by our mentor's aim,
Suspicious of his coaxing, unearned praise
And all the other unsuccessful ploys
With which he tried to justify
The ways of Milton to us boys.

The Strange Case of Julian Wright-Pratt

'Did he seem crooked? No, but then these public school and Oxford types never did. That was the whole purpose of their education, to stop them coming over as the rogues they frequently were.'
Cpt Jim Stringer in Andrew Martin, *Night Train to Jamalpur*

Money had been going missing
From trouser pockets, wallets too,
Half crowns, sixpences and shillings.
Who the thief was no-one knew.
A real mystery. How thrilling,
And yet the Head was quite unwilling
To call the local boys in blue.

He'd deal with it. Why broadcast a
Shameful secret, best kept in house?
Besides, they wouldn't solve it faster,
And their involvement might arouse
The local press. He feared disaster.
Instead he sent for our housemaster.
But would George Sellick have the nous?

And then came Wright-Pratt's disappearance.
One day he and his stuff were gone.
Purged, expunged, a midnight clearance –
No trace of Wright-Pratt lingered on.
(Except his younger brother, Clarence.)
Had he been sent home to his parents?
Of course we all guessed what he'd done.

But no official explanation
Was ever offered or proposed.
Clarence had no information,
Or so he claimed, though we supposed
His insistent protestations
Were pre-planned confabulations.
One thing was clear. The case was closed.

So it remained till decades later
When, in some meeting I was at
I asked my interlocutor
For his name. 'I'm Jules Wright-Pratt,'
He smiled, the banished perpetrator,
Alive, eyes twinkling like a satyr!
Reformed? I somehow doubted that.

A Dance to the Music of Time

Tottering, rubber-legged, through town
In shorts and hiking boots they seem
Unbalanced by their heavy rucksacks.
Bespectacled, balding pates brown
From the sun, they lean on gnarled sticks
For support, pursuing their dream
From post to way-marked wooden post
Across the country, coast to coast.

Wraith-like they march from West to East,
Through Lakeland and the Pennines, on
Towards the moors. Solitary monks
In a summer-long procession;
Some staggering wildly, like drunks,
Others mechanically plodding past,
Urged on by Alfred Wainwright's ghost,
Across the country, coast to coast.

Middle-aged men, half-way along
Their journeys. Blistered, leg-weary,
Eyes fixed abstractedly ahead,
Stoutly maintaining they're as strong
As when they started, in theory
Anyway. In practice, half-dead,
Searching for something long since lost
Across the country, coast to coast.

Grimm

How gleefully we read the announcement
Which appeared today pinned to the Palace gate,
That official type-written pronouncement
'The Prince and the Princess will separate.'

Their romance was the stuff of fairy tale –
She beautiful, though common, he, a prince.
In real life a marriage doomed to fail
We thought. (And events have proved us right since.)

They never had a chance. Affairs of state
Impinged upon them almost from the start.
Republicans among us couldn't wait
To see them come unstuck. Whatever art

She used to win him would wear off, we said.
And we were right, it very quickly did.
Long live their love? It didn't. Love lies dead.
Now Rumplestiltzkin comes to claim their kid.

The Birth of Venus

More like a frog than a Greek goddess, she
In mask and flippers floundered down the beach.
More sensible to don that diving gear
In the shallows, but she, just turned thirteen,
Only a child, plainly hadn't seen it.
And so, splay-footed, she plodded seaward,
Dredging up each footstep from the soft sand.
Despite her amphibian clumsiness
It was of Aphrodite I first thought
As she came trudging by. My glance took in
The ripening roundness of her figure,
The budding of her tiny breasts. Entranced
I watched her trek across those crowded sands,
Leaving a girl's things outgrown behind her,
Ungainly in ill-fitting womanhood.

Party Pooper

It was at the Warlock-Williams' party.
He seemed out of place, not at all 'arty',
Hardly the life and soul. Sipping a dry
Sherry he stood while I
Tried to talk to him. About my research
Mainly. Plainly it bored him, keen on church

Going, Arundel tombs, stuff like that. Phew,
It was hard work, a bit depressing too.
Death-suited, visitant, he left early.
No-one missed him really.
Poet? Misanthrope seems a synonym
More apt. God knows why they invited him.

The Potter's Wheel.

i.m. GAJ 1918–1990

I remember you at your wheel,
Centring a ball of clay
On the wheel head, gouging a well
With your thumbs, showing me the way

It was done. Squelching wetly
The clay responded, surprising
Me as, promptly, perfectly
A bowl's sides began rising.

Somehow mine weren't quite like that.
They seemed to go all wonky,
Came out either as a cow pat
Or the dong of a donkey.

'Keep trying,' I hear you say.
'Keep trying. One day you'll make one.'
You've passed them down to me, this clay
And your glaze-spattered apron.

Not Mad

Embarrassed by their father
My teenage daughters told me
Recently they'd far rather
I didn't keep them company
When we go shopping in the town.
I might, it seems, let them down
In some way. Their friends might see.
Couldn't I please cross over?

Today, wandering separately
Round the shops, we chanced to meet.
Well, no, not quite. Seeing me
Coming, they quickly crossed the street,
Avoiding an encounter.
Watching them saunter
Past, heads turned pointedly
Away, I felt obsolete.

Still, that's the way of it,
Pushed to one side we watch them pass.
Lear-like, I could rail a bit,
But what's the point? Life's farce
Not tragedy. Best face the fact
In this unfunny, final act,
Exiled, as it always is,
Love watches from across the street.

Adders Multiplying

a Prothalamion

A sudden movement, then a startling sight
There in the grass two adders reared erect,
Affording me a rare chance to inspect
Their Op-Art, zig-zag markings, black on white.
Two males then. This a mating fight.
A female waiting somewhere, I expect,
To be the victor's mate. Yes, there she lay
Basking close by. Thus male snakes, it seems, select
Which of them shall breed. To me, I must say,
It seems a rather funny way
To carry on. Still, to the serpentine
It's natural, I'm sure, to intertwine
And wrestle in these awkward, upright bouts.
The system seems to work just fine.
No adder has the slightest doubts.
Why, any other system flouts
The Laws of Nature, favouring the strong
And male adders over two feet long.

The fight proceeded, and as you'd have guessed,
The larger of the two in due course won.
The vanquished did what the vanquished have done
Down the ages – crawled off, depressed,
To hide. An angry hiss expressed
His feelings perfectly. The victor slithered on
To claim his prize. The favours of the fair
Would soon be his. His forked tongue
Flickered, sensing on the sun-warmed air
The scent of his love lying there
In the long grass. Arriving at her side
In high excitement, hurriedly he tried
To climb on top, covering her coils
With his. Perhaps I'd watch him take his bride,

I thought. But voyeurism soils
Pure passions and such moments spoils.
Best leave them to it. Watching would be wrong.
Glide on, male adder. Here I'll end my song.

The Magician's Wife

At first, baffled and wondering,
I too joined in the thundering
Applause which greeted every trick
He performed. Oh, he was magic,
Handsome and mysterious.
Naturally it got serious.
Under the Divine Afflatus
I fell. His apparatus
Impressed me. We tied the knot.
I was mistaken. We did not.
His prestidigitation
Fooled both the congregation
And me. It's one of those things,
Like interlocking Chinese rings
We came apart as easily
As abracadabra. Suddenly
He had a new blond assistant
To help him. In that instant
The illusion was over.
I saw through him as he sawed through her.

Good Grief

On our way to my brother's funeral
We called in at the Ann Summers shop.
Something strange, obviously sexual
But otherwise baffling made us stop
To buy a cock ring, some vaginal
Lubricant, handcuffs and a riding crop.

What sort of way was that to carry on
As if we frankly didn't give a toss
That my poor brother James was dead and gone?
Disgraceful! I'm completely at a loss
As to the explanation. Was there one?
Eros flicking two fingers at Thanatos?

Well, maybe so. The facts would seem to fit.
Faced with the last, the first is often strong.
It doesn't make me feel the slightest bit
Less guilty, although, as we browsed among
Those basques and pink vibrators, I'll admit
I didn't give a shit if it was wrong.

Buttons Undone

The Baron's stooge, butt of the Sisters' jokes,
That's me. I never seem to mind.
'Good old Buttons, always so kind
And gentle. One of Nature's real nice blokes...'
Well I've had enough
Of taking the rough with the rougher still.
I'll speak my piece.
OH NO YOU WON'T!
Oh yes I will.

I've been a fool, besotted by my Cinders,
Fetched and carried for the stupid cow.
And for what? You've all seen how
My chivalry crops up and hinders
A more happy end.
I'm just 'her friend.'
The part's a perfect sham.
And so am I.
OH NO YOU'RE NOT!
Oh yes I am.

Do you imagine I'm happy with my lot,
Knowing when the handsome prince arrives
Their happy-ever-after lives
Will leave mine quite unchanged? You know I'm not.
And though you'd never guess
Let me confess
Quite openly to you,
I hate the sod.
OH NO YOU DON'T!
Oh yes I do.

And as for Cinders, need I spell it out?
I'd love to get my hands on her.
So my confessions cause a stir?
You didn't think I felt like that no doubt?
Well, friends, you were wrong.
My passions are as strong
As anybody's are.
Stronger I'll bet.
OH NO THEY'RE NOT!
They are. By far!

Be honest now, convention cast aside
You know it's true. Compare
My role with his. It isn't fair.
After all, a fellow has his pride
You know, even me.
Surely I should see
For being so damn good
Some small return?
OH NO YOU SHOULDN'T!
I'm bloody sure I should.

But here comes our dungeon's ghost. Shout 'Behind you!'
And I will ask you where, then turn
Too late to see him. I never learn.
Next time don't let me have to remind you.
He's coming, is he?
Well, get busy.
What's that? The ghost is here? Where?
I can't see him.
BEHIND YOU! BEHIND YOU!
Where? There's nothing there.

Poor Poets

'Great poets and great sages draw no prize
With women.'
George Meredith, *Modern Love*

They don't want poets. They want wealthy crooks,
Rich businessmen and others of that ilk.
Slim volumes can't compete with fat cheque books.

Most women cannot wait to get their hooks
Into a chap who'll buy them furs and silk.
They don't want poets. They want wealthy crooks

Whose money guarantees they'll keep their looks
And won't end up grizzled like Acker Bilk.
Slim volumes can't compete with fat cheque books.

A wealthy spouse ensures they can cock snooks
At those who haven't bathed in asses' milk.
They don't want poets. They want wealthy crooks

Who'll hire them chauffeurs, masseurs, maids and cooks
And never ever quote from Proust or Rilke.
Slim volumes can't compete with fat cheque books.

To me this Mating Game, this sex thing, sucks.
Our score, as wordsmiths? A resounding zilch!
They don't want poets. They want wealthy crooks.
Slim volumes can't compete with fat cheque books.

Bye Bye Love

I am not sure I want another chance.
With few regrets I'll watch love fade away.
Goodbye to passion, farewell to romance,
I'm finished with all that I'm pleased to say.

With few regrets I'll watch love fade away.
It's sad somehow, but still, it had to be.
I'm finished with all that. I'm pleased to say
Goodbye to love at last. I've been set free.

It's sad somehow. But still it had to be –
It was only illusion after all.
Goodbye to love. At last I've been set free.
It didn't last. (It doesn't, I recall.)

It was only illusion after all,
And yet it's hard to bid it all adieu.
It didn't last. It doesn't. I recall
That I'm resolved on what I have to do.

And yet it's hard to bid it all adieu.
Goodbye to passion? Farewell to romance?
That I'm resolved on what I have to do
I am not sure. I want another chance.

Cornermen

Helpless, disabled by his bandaged hands
And eight ounce gloves, he depends on them.
He does the fighting but they take care of him,
Fussing like new parents over their first born.

Slumped on his stool, he watches them at work.
They know what's needed. One of them removes
His gumshield, holds the bottle while he swigs,
The bucket while he spits. The other smooths

Vaseline on his temples, pokes a bud
Gingerly up his nose. To them it's clear.
'Jab and move,' they tell him, coaxing him,
Trapped like a toddler in its high chair,

To take a spoonful of advice. 'Come on,'
They urge, 'jab and move.' Their words betray
A slight impatience with this wayward child
Who won't do as he's told. 'Seconds away...'

A voice orders, and feeding him his gumshield
They clamber through the ropes. 'Jab and move,'
They remind him, lingering on the ring apron,
Watching him rise with something like love.

For Georgie on Burns Night

A pugilist, my youngest daughter,
At ten year old. I hadnae thought her
The sort who would not ask for quarter
Or seek a truce,
But battle on, as fighters ought'er,
Though she turn puce.

Aye, even trapped like wee Jack Horner,
When shipping punches in the corner,
The heat turned up as in a sauna,
She does not drop;
For holding, though the ref may warn her,
She'll cover up

Till she can turn the opposition
To trap them in the same position,
Pursuing what's her final mission,
Her stated aim,
To pummel them into submission,
The true end-game.

Och, Georgie, aye, I always knew it,
Deep in my bones seemed to intuit
One day they'd let young ladies do it,
The Noble Art,
Now daughter raise the name of Jowett
To stand apart.

I couldnae. Soft as avocado,
My fighting talk was all bravado.
The little maids from the Mikado
Had got more balls.
I was a loser, just a saddo,
The truth appals.

Now is your time. So up and at 'em,
Arms flailing like the Mighty Atom.
Five daughters, and though I begat 'em
All, I'd not guessed
Ye'd be the fighter. That's the datum.
Your Da's impressed!

Blow by Blow

'What has been missing in the past is a local fighter to draw the public back to boxing in Middlesbrough and in Brian Graham I have found one.'
John Spensley, Boxing Manager and Promoter

Round One

He sat beside us in the balcony,
Bristling and belligerent, denim-clad,
Nursing a pint. Suddenly he turned to me
And spoke, speech slurred. 'This next fight on's my lad.'
(Candidly I wondered if perhaps he'd had
One too many?) 'Pardon?' 'His Da I am.'
'I'm sorry?' 'This next fight on. I'm his dad.'
'Your son, is it?' He pointed at my programme,
'That's him. That's our lad.' 'Which? That one? Brian Graham?'

It seemed only polite to then enquire
If he was any good. 'Shit hot. You'll see.'
We doubted that, thought Dad perhaps a liar
(Well, he'd stick up for his son naturally.)
Nodding, we smiled at him indulgently,
Prepared to humour him. And here they came,
The fighters. Would the lad turn out to be
Another disappointment, a source of shame,
Or would he justify that proud, parental claim?

All over in two rounds, the crowd went wild.
A football chant sprang up. We joined in.
'There's only one Brian Graham!' Brian's Da smiled,
Accepting all our tributes with a grin.
He turned to us and spoke above the din,
'They've never had no time for us.' (He meant
His neighbours.) 'They think we're shit, the effin'
Bastards. Well bugger them!' He was content
Now in the knowledge Brian's victory was sent

To turn the tables on them and restore
The name of Graham and the family pride.
'He'll make 'em give us some respect, I'm sure
'E will.' It must have seemed to him the tide
Had turned at last, that Brian's victory supplied
A hope of better things. As you'd expect,
We didn't argue, wouldn't dare have tried.
(Sheer cowardice on our part, I suspect.)
Two rounds and already Brian had won our respect.

Round Two

Next day the local paper ran the story.
'TRIUMPHANT DEBUT FOR MIDDLESBROUGH PRO.'
(Dad no doubt basked in the reflected glory.)
The article alongside Brian's photo
Told how he'd been involved ten years ago
In a childhood accident. Badly burned,
Electrocuted, it was touch and go
At first. But he'd pulled through, then slowly learned
To use his arms again as surgery had turned

His back and shoulders to a patchwork quilt.
(I'd seen the scars in the ring the night before.)
Hospitalised while the surgeons rebuilt
What 11,000 volts had seared, Brian swore
He'd make a full recovery, seemed sure
He'd battle back till he was fully fit.
Two years he clung to that belief. What's more
He never for a moment doubted it.
Despite the awful pain, young Brian wouldn't quit.

Discharged at last he started to work out,
Then took up boxing in a local gym.
A natural, he never knew self-doubt,
With confidence full to the very brim.
The other kids were soon in awe of him.
He's run up seventeen victories on the trot,
(Opponents had two chances – none and slim)
Before deciding to turn pro. A shot
At the title his ultimate goal. And why not?

They gave the last word to his manager
Who acknowledged Brian's drawing power
And punch, but foresaw a real danger.
'He hits so hard he's broken bones before
In both his hands.' He concluded that 'our
Brian' had a real chance. No denying
His punches put opponents on the floor.
The word that sprang to mind, although I'm trying
Not to say it, reading all this? Electrifying!

Round Three

I'm not the first by any means to share
A love of boxing and of poetry.
No boxer/writers are by no means rare,
I share a long, illustrious ancestry –
George Bernard Shaw, Gene Tunney and Lord B
To name a few. In the modern annal,
The one we're still compiling currently,
The prime example must be Vernon Scannel,
Ex-pug and fine poet. (And that's not just flannel.)

I'm not like him. I never was a pro.
I boxed at school but wasn't good enough
To make a go of it. Modest? Hell, no.
Though by our peers we were considered tough,
The truth is we weren't made of sterner stuff
At all. And if perhaps you're wondering why
I took it up, the art of fisticuffs,
I'll tell you. In winter we kept warm and dry
Inside the school gymnasium. A boy could die

Cross-country running out on Hampstead Heath,
Or playing soccer in the wind and rain.
Who wants a runny nose and chattering teeth?
For outdoor sports you had to be insane.
Far better box. A boy must use his brain.
Besides, like Martin Luther King, I had a dream,
A family tradition to maintain.
My brothers both had led the boxing team
And so must I, I thought. (How foolish now they seem

The ambitions of our youth.) Still, they explain
Why I began to box. I loved it too
And didn't mind the bruises or the pain
When some kid's long left hand came snaking through
My guard. I wore those bruises, black and blue,
Like campaign medals, with a soldier's pride.
Silly? I know it is, and yet it's true
Boxing somehow made me feel good inside,
Though why that should be so, like you, I'm mystified.

All this, of course, was thirty years ago.
I haven't laced the gloves on since that time.
At least, unlike George Foreman though, I know
(How can I put it?) that I'm past my prime,
Well past it. I'll admit the fact that I'm
Not young enough or fit enough to fight. Okay?
(You'd think that growing older was a crime.
It takes a brave man nowadays to say
'That's it. I quit. Time to admit, I've had my day.')

I'm still a fight fan. In the cheaper seats
At shows throughout the North I can be found.
For sheer excitement I've found nothing beats
A grandstand finish in the final round
As two men slug it out. Then, at the sound
Of the bell, instantly the action ends
And grinning hugely, with their arms around
Each other, former foes become firm friends.
It's funny how cathartic a good punch-up tends

To be. For purged of all hostility,
It leaves us cleansed and calm, our faith restored
In man and his innate nobility.
At times I have been moved and even awed
By what I've seen. And could I but record
The heroism I have seen displayed
In the ring, my work's success would be assured.
If I could get it down I'd have it made.
Unfortunately it's not that easy I'm afraid.

Still, even so, when I began to seek
A subject I could write about in verse,
A subject with the right sort of mystique,
I turned to boxing. Yes, I could do worse
I thought than chronicle the sad reverse
In Ali's fortunes. Poor old Muhammad!
How hard-earned every million dollar purse.
(He paid full price for all the fights he had.)
I had a working title to – the Aliad.

But that is not my story I've decided,
For Ali has been hymned by better men.
Bud Schulberg, Jose Torres have provided
Far better tributes than my ball point pen
Could manage. I had better think again.
Some local hero who has been neglected
And overlooked till now. But who? And then,
Suddenly inspired, I recollected
Brian Graham. The perfect choice, I reflected.

The more I mused the more I was convinced
That Brian's story is the one for me.
A short and simple tale, yet it evinced
All that is best in us as you shall see.
And unlike Rocky I or II or III,
It's true. I swear it is, every single word,
Packed with pathos, rich in humanity.
So let me tell you simply what occurred,
A tale the like of which you've never heard.

Round Four

Things weren't so easy for him next time out,
In Hartlepool's exquisite Borough Hall.
The North East's finest venue, without doubt,
Packed with our Brian's supporters wall to wall.
Dad spruce and smart at ringside, I recall,
Leapt up as Brian entered and embraced him.
Quite what Pete Lock from London made of all
This, who knows? (Not that Brian's dad disgraced him.
Far from it.) As Brian climbed in the ring to face him,

Acknowledging the cheers which now rang out,
Lock looked across and spat dismissively.
'Gentlemen, please. Next a middleweight bout
Between, in the red corner...' The MC
Introduced Lock first. Brian sportingly
Led the applause for his opponent. 'And
In the blue corner, from Middlesbrough...' Suddenly
A roar went up, spontaneous, unplanned,
Deafening. Brian bowed, acknowledging the hand,

'Brian Graham!' As the noise subsided
The ref called them to the centre of the ring.
They listened while he hurriedly provided
His instructions. Then, to their corners turning,
Abandoned by their handlers, standing
Alone, the fighters waited for the bell.
Nervous now, no-one had the heart to sing
And precious few to shout or cheer or yell.
For what would happen when the bell went, who could tell?

Round one began and Brian advanced on Lock.
They circled one another. Suddenly
Lock's right shot out and Brian went down. The shock
Was too much for us fight fans. Silently
We watched as Brian rose up on one knee
And waited till the count reached eight to rise.
Lock piled in, of course, scenting victory,
Threw wild rights designed to capitalise
On that one lucky punch. Brian covered up. Ringwise,

He knew he'd got to dig himself well in,
Defend until his brain began to clear.
He mustn't let Lock hit him on the chin
Again. (Defeat had never seemed so near.)
A pile driver right whistled round his ear.
Tucked in behind his guard, Brian waited
And watched as Lock punched on, his sole idea
To knock Brian out. At last the storm abated.
Lock was clearly tiring. His strength had dissipated.

Now Brian began to counter. At the bell
One felt perhaps he might be coming back.
Round two confirmed the hope. Although he still
Boxed cautiously, defence turned to attack.
Now it was Pete Lock's turn to face the flack.
He wilted as the second round wore on.
He'd shot his bolt. His own defence seemed slack.
He'd nothing left at all. The lad was gone.
The crowd and Brian's corner loudly urged him on.

Round three, and Brian came out like a tank,
Determined if he could to finish it.
A round house left, and to his knees Lock sank.
He struggled up at five, both brave and fit,
And raised his guard, but Brian simply hit
Him with a body shot and down he went
Again. He rose at six, but Brian had the bit
Between his teeth and as a left hook sent
Him to the floor, to save him further punishment,

The ref called a halt. Brian punched the air
In triumph, while, ringside, the crowd went wild.
His seconds tumbled through the ropes to share
The victory. Into the ring they piled,
Eager to embrace him. Brian just smiled,
Fought free of them, keen to commiserate
With his opponent first and be reconciled.
(The celebrations after all could wait.)
He crossed the ring to Lock's corner. 'You alright, mate?'

Lock looked up from his stool and winked one eye,
As Brian bent to hug him like a friend.
The two embraced, swapped compliments, while I
Opened my programme so I could append
A few brief words recalling how the end
Had come. 'KO Round 3,' was all I wrote.
I noticed the promoter too had penned
A self-explanatory programme note,
Designed, obviously, to publicise and promote

His fighter's links with his new local sponsors.
'Brian Graham is sponsored by...' it said,
'J and S Fletcher, Building Contractors.'
Perhaps more appropriate, I thought, as I read
That and watched Brian as he gently led
His opponent round the ring, his arm wrapped
Protectively round the man he'd hammered,
(In tribute to them how we cheered and clapped)
Would be a demolition firm. Yes, far more apt.

Round Five

Collecting with a bucket for MENCAP
In the interval our Brian reappeared.
He moved along the rows until the chap
Beside me called out to him as he neared,
'Would you sign this for me, Brian?' Brian steered
Towards us, took the programme and the Bic
Biro. 'So what's your name?' he enquired,
Pen poised to write. 'If you'd just put to Vic.
That's V- I- C.' Brian laughed. 'Fighters aren't all fick!'

Round Six

Just one month later in his third pro fight,
At Middlesbrough Town Hall, Brian topped the bill.
Rumour had it that a London date might
Follow if he continued to fulfil
His early promise with a third quick kill.
Some said Mickey Duff had shown an interest,
That fame and fortune were beckoning. Still,
First Joe Dean from Huddersfield, the best
Fighter he'd faced so far, would pose the perfect test.

And so he did. He put up stern resistance
And showed us fans that he could box a bit.
In fact, Joe Dean survived and went the distance,
The first of Brian's opponent not to quit
Before the final bell. Difficult to hit,
He forced our Brian to box and use his brain,
And biased as we were, we had to admit
Put up a splendid show. Still it was plain
By the end that Brian, on points, had won again.

Oh how we cheered the verdict. What a fight!
A packed house and a profitable show.
The bar takings were well up. A great night,
The first, we hoped, of many. Even Joe
Received a big hand as he turned to go,
The racist taunts with which he'd been greeted
Forgotten. He'd done alright. Time to show
A bit of appreciation. Defeated
Joe Dean with magnanimity could be treated.

What we didn't know then and couldn't guess
Was that Joe had fractured Brian's cheekbone.
Two days later the local sporting press
Broke the story. Handicapped from round one
By the injury, all agreed he'd shown
Real courage. But the broken bone would mean
He couldn't fight again for months. He'd done
His work a little too well, had Joe Dean.
A bit of bad luck. The injury an unforeseen

Hold-up to Brian's blossoming career.
Still, that was boxing, and we had no doubt
That he'd be back. No, that was crystal clear.
Brian Graham would not be counted out,
Not him. No chance. For it was all about
Determination. Brian would attack.
He'd get up from misfortune's latest clout,
Then like a freight train he'd some storming back!
Resilience was one thing Brian didn't lack.

Round Seven

Five months later the first posters appeared
Announcing Brian Graham's comeback fight.
At Gaskins Night Club, Thursday April third,
Against Blackpool's Billy Hill. It was quite
A step-up. Though not exactly top-flight,
His opponent was a top twenty rated
British Middleweight. To scale those dizzy heights
Was still Brian's dream, till now frustrated.
But now the chance had come. His destiny awaited.

But then, ten days before the fight was due,
The day before a boxing/dinner show
At the Northern Sporting Club, (a black tie 'do')
Brian's name was added to the bill. A no
Risk exercise, a warm-up fight. Although
His opponent had had three pro bouts,
He hadn't won one yet. A novice pro.
A real mismatch. I had serious doubts
That it could last more than a round or thereabouts.

Round Eight

Their dining done, the members waited for
The boxing to begin. (How big the ring
Seemed, erected on the ballroom dance floor.)
Some gestured for the wine waiter to bring
Another brandy, or leaned back puffing
On Churchillian cigars. Clouds of smoke
Drifted in the glare of the ring lighting,
While through the buzz of conversation broke
A loud guffaw as someone told a crude, blue joke.

Up there in the ring, like a silent sentry,
The MC dumbly waited. Not long to go.
He fiddled with his mic. The fighters' entry
Must be imminent. And here they came now.
Unaccustomed to opening the show,
Brian Graham strode swiftly down the aisle.
Relaxed and confident, he seemed to know,
As he ducked between the ropes with a smile
That tonight's bout wouldn't prove much of a trial.

Now chatting happily to his seconds
He awaited Jerry Golden's arrival.
(Around the ring those in the know reckoned
Golden wouldn't prove much of a rival.
He'd little chance even of survival.)
And here he came. No doubt the lad had tried
As every real fighter must, to stifle
His fears, but he still appeared half-terrified.
At best a work-out would be all he could provide.

‘Gentlemen, please...’ The MC had to wait
A moment for the hubbub to subside.
‘A four round contest, made at Middleweight,
Between and introducing, on my left hand side,
In the red corner, from Manchester’s Moss Side,
Jerry Golden.’ Lukewarm, sparse applause. ‘And
His opponent tonight, from Teesside,
Brian Graham.’ A slightly better hand,
Though nothing like the home town welcome he’d command

Next week in the Boro. Introductions
Over, the fighters joined the referee
To hear the familiar instructions.
‘Keep them up, break when you’re told. Let’s see
A good clean fight. Shake hands.’ The customary
Touching of gloves to wish each other well,
Then to their corners momentarily
Turning, like prisoners in a condemned cell,
They waited nervously for the opening bell.

Ding! As threatening as a frightened rabbit
Poor Jerry Golden made himself advance.
He seemed to know instinctively he’d had it,
He clearly didn’t feel he had a chance.
He tried a light left jab. It seemed to glance
Off Brian’s face innocuously enough.
Astonished, the audience looked on askance
As Brian went down from this powder puff
Of a punch, cradling his face in a crimson glove.

What was wrong? 'Five...Six...' the ref counted on
Till Brian struggled to his feet, his face
Disfigured, the sight in his right eye gone,
His features twisted in a pained grimace.
His plight was obvious. The ref's embrace,
Signalling to all that the fight was over,
A formality. Gesturing, in case
Precious time was lost, for the ringside doctor,
The ref led Brian gently back to his corner.

It couldn't, could it, be just plain bad luck,
The cheekbone gone again? We began to fear
There must be more to it than that. What struck
Us was the fact that Brian did appear
Prone to bone injuries. We'd an idea
That in some way that childhood accident
Might be to blame. We weren't exactly clear
How or why, and yet it seemed self-evident
To us that massive shock must be significant.

Meanwhile Jerry Golden celebrated
His first, most unexpected victory.
Our Brian, of course, was devastated,
Sitting on his stool disconsolately
While the doctor examined the injury;
The latest in a list too long to log
That spelled the end of his career, surely?
A crippling, portentous catalogue
That cast Brian as the eternal underdog.

Round Nine

'BOXER BRIAN GRAHAM QUITS.' The headline
Ten days later confirmed what we had feared.
It seems he had no choice but to consign
His dreams to the dustbin, for it appeared
From tests his bones were weak. If he persevered
With boxing, inevitably it meant
More injuries. Effectively cashiered,
(No-one willingly risks disfigurement)
Brian, aged twenty four, had announced his retirement.

His short career was over and his dream
To be a champ would never be realised.
He had the heart and skill, but it would seem
Not the bones. What the doctors had advised
He knew he must accept. The things he prized,
They'd told him plainly, he could not attain.
His hopes and dreams would have to be revised.
He still loved the sport, but it was certain
Though he might coach youngsters, he'd never fight again.

All over. That was it. Brian had fought
And lost his final battle. Time to quit.
Thanking his loyal fans for their support,
Brian bade boxing a fond farewell. It
Obviously upset him quite a bit
But, uncomplaining, Brian took it on the chin.
KO'd by Fate, for once forced to admit
Defeat, he didn't whine or wallow in
Self-pity. What was the point? He knew he couldn't win?

Round Ten

A comeback? Not a chance, and yet there was
Some talk of one months later in the press.
It seems the rumours all arose because
A second doctor, asked to reassess
Brian's case, suggested a simple, less
Gloomy prognosis. Perhaps he'd fought too soon,
Before he'd healed properly? The process
Now complete, a comeback in May or June,
Under new management, needn't be inopportune.

Pictured training to be a pub landlord,
No wonder Brian dreamed of a return.
He looked embarrassed and a little bored,
Though no doubt he was keen enough to learn
The licensing trade. Easy to discern
There might be problems. Plainly, for a start,
Every would-be hard man, eager to earn
That tag, at chucking-out time would get smart
With him. He'd face a threat from every young upstart.

He'd have no choice. He'd have to put them out,
Each drunken thug, each violent maniac.
He'd know too much for them without a doubt,
But there'd be others keen to have a crack.
(Of hard men in the Boro there's no lack.)
To him they'd be a constant irritation.
No wonder he still dreamed of a comeback.
But in spite of that second opinion
Brian's hopes of a return proved an illusion.

Round Eleven

Last time I saw him, it was four years later.
A boxing show in Marton. Brought back to test
Another up and coming gladiator,
Joe Dean was fighting. Midway through the first
I noticed, near the back, watching unimpressed,
Stood Brian Graham. Ignored by the fans
He watched his former foe, now past his best,
Struggling, from the moment the fight began,
Bravely but vainly, to contain the younger man.

Joe backed into the ropes. Forced to retreat,
He covered up before each fresh assault.
His only goal was to postpone defeat.
But as the rounds wore on he seemed to wilt.
Half-way through the fifth, the ref called a halt
And mercifully pulled him from the fray.
He'd seen enough. It wasn't anybody's fault.
The simple truth was Joe had had his day.
Smiling ruefully to himself, Brian turned away.

Round Twelve

Well, that's it. That's my story. What a tale.
Dramatic, poignant, tragic and all true.
I really cannot see how it can fail,
But then I wrote it. Let me ask, can you?
You've got some reservations? Just a few?
Some come on then, let's hear your argument.
You don't like rhyme? Oh, in its place you do?
But mine didn't add to your enjoyment,
You felt it slowed the action up to some extent?

You may be right, and yet I must confess
Your reservations cause me no unease.
What would cause me considerable distress
Would be to find that Brian Graham agrees
With you. What he'll feel when he finally sees
My opus is a mystery. In fact,
Although my aim has simply been to please,
I've no idea at all how he'll react.
I hope, of course, that he'll be flattered and gobsmacked

He might instead decide to sue for libel.
(Though any claim he makes will be defended.)
The whole thing's true, I swear it on the Bible.
(And every error in it's been amended.)
Besides of which, no libel was intended.
How he'll take it, I'll have to wait and see.
I do hope though, that Brian's not offended
And that he's fairly fond of poetry
And doesn't really want to take a swing at me.

Notes

Stanza 1
West Cornforth, County Durham, 22 August 1978.

Stanza 4
A passer-by told this constable they had seen a stocky, middle-aged man exiting the lane in the early hours of the morning. Unfortunately, the officer failed to take down his details, and despite repeated public appeals, the witness never came forward.

Stanza 23
Clayton Whittaker was appointed Acting Head of Durham CID just weeks before the discovery of Miriam's body.

Stanza 39
Teesside Crown Court, 16 July 1979.

Stanza 50
The Northern Echo, 21August, 2004.

Stanza 51
These further charges were mentioned in the press reports of Lawrence's suicide, and can only have been leaked to the local press by the police.

Acknowledgements

Acknowledgements are due to the editors of the following publications and periodicals in which some of these poems first appeared – *The Countryman, Iron, Other Poetry, Outposts, Poetry Review, the Spectator* and *the Yorkshire Journal*; *Northern Poetry Two* (Littlewood/Arc, 1991), Andy Croft and Sue Dymoke (eds) *Not Just a Game* (Five Leaves, 2006) and *Sketches* (Wolds Print, 2015). Some of these poems were also published in the pamphlets *Blow by Blow* (Mudfog 1996) and *The Old Campaigners* (Redbeck 2001).